We Are Never Alone

Norma L. Baker

PublishAmerica
Baltimore

First printing

ISBN: 1-4241-8656-0

PUBLISHED BY PUBLISHAMERICA, LLLP

www.publishamerica.com

Baltimore

Printed in the United States of America

Dedicated to my daughters. They are my inspiration. God is our refuge and strength, a very present help in time of trouble. Psalm 46:1

Foreword

Life has many peaks and valleys. Growing up I was a tiny girl and a little on the shy side. Because of my stature throughout my childhood and teen years, I acquired a few nicknames: spider legs, little bit, and mutt. The first twelve years of my life we lived in a rural area in Arkansas. My dad was a carpenter by trade; work was slow where we lived, so in order for him to have jobs we moved to Missouri where construction was in demand.

Coming from Arkansas I had a little accent, mostly hillbilly sounding. I didn't realize this until I started in a new school. The kids made fun of the way I talked. This hurt my feelings and, because of being different, I refused to talk for a couple weeks. I began to practice how I spoke and not to say, "y'all."

Innocence of childhood, lack of self-confidence as a teenager, slow to maturity, these were the challenges early in my life. Each of us has a particular gift from God; we are all different and special in our own way. It is a journey finding the plan God has for you.

When you think you have the future all planned out, the unpredictable can happen. Mine followed the unpredictable. Married at the age of nineteen, life just couldn't seem to get any better. I had high expectations for a long and happy life. As it turned out it was short term. Tragedy, divorce, and broken relationships were my destiny.

I want to share my experiences, learning to deal with all the peaks and valleys, growing in strength, faith, and coping with the challenges I had to face. There were times when I lost faith and took matters into my own hands, making many wrong decisions.

My hope is that others can relate to what I went through and perhaps find some comfort and meaning.

My Life's Journey: Finding Your Own Purpose and Identity

Suddenly you're single. It could be late in life or after a few years of marriage either from death or divorce. What do you do? Are you prepared? Do you have work experience or an education to go out into the workplace to earn a living? Many do not. Age can be a factor and those who have been housewives find it difficult to get back into the workplace. Being a single parent comes with challenges, both financially and emotionally. What do you do?

In situations like this many rush into another marriage for security reasons, not fully taking the time to know what you want for yourself. Is this person right for me?

Will it be a lasting relationship? I'm sure we all have heard the phrase, you must first take care of yourself, be a positive person, and know what you want out of life. In order to have better relationships and be confident to go after jobs you have to feel good about you.

I've been through marriages, divorces, and relationships, all the while trying to figure out what I wanted. A lot of mistakes were made. I had to make a career for myself; along the way I had some great jobs, and some were just okay. My earlier experience had been in retail; that is where I started. Each time I got a different job it was a step up. It took awhile until I finally was able to say I had a career.

Go back and look at your childhood. Look deep into your soul and find the childhood attributes that make you what you are today. What we were as children made us what we are today. Those are your strong points. Growing up I was the middle child between two sisters, two years' difference from the oldest, and five years from the youngest. I remember my oldest sister and I fought a lot.

My younger sister was too small to play with, so I spent most of my time playing alone. I didn't mind. I would pretend and had a great imagination, was creative, and organized everything! Those traits stayed with me all my life and carried over into my career. I believe that is why I can be alone and be happy.

Life can be simple. I grew up on a farm in Arkansas living the simple life. Our home was ten miles from town. My oldest sister and I walked one mile to catch the bus to school, no matter what the weather. There were plenty of snowy and cold days. At age nine I wanted to take piano lessons, but the only piano teacher lived in town. During the school year I would walk to her house to take my lesson during the lunch hour. The lessons cost only fifty cents! During the summer months I would walk the mile to the highway and catch a ride with the mailman. We had nothing to worry about; crime was unheard of. This was a safe place to live.

We attended a small country church. All of the men wore overalls, most were farmers, and the women as well as the girls, wore cotton dresses. Unlike today, women never wore slacks to church; it was not proper. Every spring there was a revival meeting at the church. At one particular revival I was eight years old and became aware that I was a sinner. I wanted to be saved. One night I went up for the altar call and surrendered my life to Jesus. The pastor and members knelt down and prayed with me, and I was overcome with joy in my heart. I cried and laughed at the same time! I remember my mother shouting and dancing in the aisle. I didn't know what she was doing until later when I learned it was because she was happy. Getting baptized was the next step. Our belief was to be immersed under water, and the only place for that was a creek nearby.

The following Sunday afternoon I was baptized along with several others. I was so short I had to stand on the foot of the pastor and on my tiptoes at that! I do remember the feeling of happiness and joy afterwards.

On the farm I had a lot of space to play. One of the things I loved playing as a child was building a playhouse in the back yard under this big oak tree. We used wood to heat our home, and there were stacks of wood. I took wood logs and made an outline for the walls, found things for furniture, and played for hours. Another favorite pastime was to climb a big sycamore tree. The branches were low to the ground, and I would climb up as far as I felt comfortable, then pretend I was a princess and this was my tower where I could look out and see far away. There were plenty of blackberry patches on our property, and when the blackberries were ripe and ready to pick, we would pick berries by the gallon to sell them. This was the way my sisters and I earned money for the county fair.

Having been sheltered all my life from wordily things, leaving home would be somewhat intimidating. The life I grew up in revolved around religion; we were not allowed to participate in a lot of activities outside of the church, which is not a bad thing, but I did not learn a lot about life. In high school I only had a few dates. My maturity level was low and I was naïve about a lot of things.

My Story

My first marriage was right out of college. I attended a Baptist College in the Midwest. I adjusted well to college, enjoying freedom I never had before and was excited to make my own choices. Going off to college was the first time I had been away from home for any length of time.

On the drive I was quiet and didn't say much; this wasn't unusual for me. The thoughts going thru my mind were a bit scary, not knowing what lay ahead, who would my roommate be, if we would like each other, and if I would get homesick. Tears swelled up in my eyes, and my throat felt tight, but I did not want my parents to know how I was feeling. On the other hand, I was a bit excited for a new adventure. There was a lot of growing up to do. I began to wonder if maybe I really could have a career and do something with my life. The confidence and self-esteem wasn't there. I was always saying I couldn't. My major was music, and my desire was to be a music teacher.

Life in the dorm was different from anything I had experienced before. Luck was on my side. Shortly after I unpacked, my roommate arrived. She came bouncing in. We exchanged greetings and were excited about living together for the next couple years.

With her bubbly personality we clicked immediately. After exchanging information about ourselves we found out we only lived thirty miles from each other. Small world! We were both petite close to the same stature and wore the same clothing size.

The girl's dorm was connected to the cafeteria; this was great. If it were cold or raining we would not have to go outside to get there. The foyer of the cafeteria was glassed in, a place where everyone waited until the doors were open to enter. You were not allowed to go inside until five minutes before meals. It became a place to mingle and meet other students. After several days I began to notice this one particular guy sitting on the ledge of the glass wall. He didn't seem to mingle, and one day I walked over and started a conversation with him. His name was Stanley. He was six foot two inches, here on a basketball scholarship, playing for the varsity team. From that time on he came looking for me. One day he got up enough courage to ask me out on a date. After meeting Stanley everything changed. All I thought about was getting married. He was the first person I had a real relationship with. In high school I had boyfriends and crushes but never a one-on-one relationship. This was the beginning of a long relationship.

As a teenager he loved to work on cars. He had bought an old coupe that needed a lot of repairs to even get it running. He spent all his time working on this car, putting a new motor in, getting all the parts that were needed, shining it up, and painting it bright turquoise. It ran really well, and he loved showing it off! Besides working on cars, he also raced stock cars at a track near his hometown. In high school he was the star basketball player. He had a pretty good life. I guess you could say he was the All-American boy.

The first semester of college went by rather quickly. We were together constantly. For Christmas Stanley decided to ask me to marry him. The plan was to go out to the park, which was a hangout for college students, take a walk around the small lake, and then pop the question. Needless to say I accepted and thought life could not get any better. A wedding was planned for the summer following graduation.

Making plans for the summer months I signed up for a summer mission program sponsored by the Southern Baptists. It would be ten weeks of going into the rural communities and helping with Vacation Bible School and Youth Camp. A small salary would be paid at the end of the ten weeks. The summer was over before I knew it, but the experience was spiritually uplifting.

September came. Students were hustling about campus, enrolling in classes, looking for a familiar face, and anticipating a great year. New students were finding their way around campus. Because of his grades, Stanley lost his basketball scholarship after the first semester of the second year. He dropped out of college at mid-term to begin working so we could get married in July. This went over like a lead balloon with his parents, but he had his mind made up, and nothing was going to change it. He applied for a job in Kansas City with a refrigeration company. He began work and joined the union as an apprentice-in-training, a repairman working toward a journeyman position, which would take five years.

I was in the second semester of my last year. One night I had a dream; it was very disturbing and real. In the dream a person was lying on a bed covered with a white sheet, the face not visible. I was sitting beside the bed repeating a Bible verse to this person, but could not see a face. I kept repeating over and over, saying, "Read Malachi 1:5."

The floor was filled with fog that came up around my ankles. Attending a religious-based college, everyone was required to take a course in the Old Testament and The New Testament. Although I studied the Old Testament, I knew very little about the book of Malachi. Waking up I was in a cold sweat and sat straight up in bed. The first thing I did was find my Bible and look up this verse of scripture I kept repeating. It referred to God's love for Jacob and something about an eye. What did this mean? I was disturbed and could not get it out of my head. I spoke to the dorm mom and told the dream to her.

Mom was a wise person and everyone loved her. She was kind and gentle in every way. The advice was to put it in the back of your mind and do not dwell on it. God was preparing me for something in the future. I would know when the time came. We prayed and I felt much better. I was able to forget it for a while, remembering from time to time.

Graduation day finally came, but it was bittersweet. I was excited about the wedding only a month away, but leaving friends I'd spent the last two years with was sad.

We shared a lot of hugs and tears saying goodbye. Some friends I would never see again.

The wedding date was July 4, 1959, and it took place in a small country church. It was attended by family and friends. I wasn't familiar with planning a formal wedding, so ours was simple and informal. Stanley's employment was in Kansas City, so immediately after the reception we took off to begin our life. He found a three-room apartment and had it all ready for us. One of the first things we did was find a church. Stanley was of the same faith; basically we would be living the same lifestyle I grew up in.

City life was exciting! I had always dreamed about living somewhere other than on a farm. Kansas City was the largest city I had ever seen. I adjusted well! Four months into our marriage I became pregnant. Stanley enjoyed his work and doing well. Our first daughter, Janet, was born August 11, 1960.

A couple of years went by. Our apartment became a little cramped, so we decided to look into buying a house. We got in touch with a realtor, and we began to look at houses. After seeing the third house, we immediately fell in love with it. This is the one! A contract was signed, and within a week the realtor called to say our offer had been accepted and the loan was in the works. Thirty days later we closed on the house.

How exciting! The next thing was to get insurance. While discussing the homeowners insurance, it was suggested we add disability insurance, should something happen to Stanley the house payment would be covered. Little did we know how important this would be for us. God works in our lives even when we are not aware.

We moved into our house with all the excitement new homeowners have. It had a big backyard where Janet could run and play. The hardwood floors were beautiful.

Everything was going great! Thirty days later, April 30, 1962 our world changed forever. Things can change in an instant. Stanley went to work as usual. By 9:00 a.m. I received a phone call that Stanley had an accident at work and was being taken to the hospital. Someone was coming to pick me up and take me there. When I asked how bad he was, the only answer I got was, "It's not good." I wasn't given any more information. Needless to say, I was very nervous not knowing the extent of his injury.

All sorts of things were running through my mind trying to figure out what could have happened. It was nothing compared to what I was about to experience.

As I entered the hospital, I was directed where to go. Walking down this long hallway I looked near the elevator and saw a hospital cart with a person lying on it covered with a white sheet. I could not see a face. I began to run! At that moment my dream came back to me, remembering being counseled that when the time came I would know. As I turned the corner it was Stanley. I lost it! I fell over his unconscious body sobbing uncontrollably. They were waiting for the elevator to take him to surgery. It was fate that I arrived at that moment; in just a few seconds he would have been on the elevator and gone. God's timing is perfect.

I was taken into a small room so I could regain my composure. After a few minutes I stopped crying, and I learned what happened. Stanley removed a compressor from a refrigerator and placed it in the middle of the room to work on it. After making a few adjustments, he walked over to plug it into the wall socket. When he turned on the power switch the compressor blew up instantly. Stanley was hit by a piece of metal and was knocked unconscious to the floor, blood flowing from his head.

The hospital staff was very kind and sympathetic toward me. I was taken to a waiting room and asked if there was anything they could do. The TV news had already picked up the story and a broadcaster reported it on the morning news. A former pastor from the Church we moved from a month ago saw the news, and within a short period of time walked in the door. I was so relived to see him. As he took my hands in his we began to pray. I was totally in God's hand now. The poem "Footprints" fit the occasion. I could not walk; God was carrying me. After we prayed, the pastor called one of the church members and asked them to begin a prayer chain. This went on all day. There is power in prayer.

After about an hour the doctor came into the waiting room. He asked for me, and I acknowledged him. I had been told he was one of the best in his field. I must have looked very fragile. I was only 22 years old, petite, and looked younger than my age.

There was compassion for me. I was so impressed! The extent of his injury was explained to me. A piece of steel four inches long had gone through his right eye and lodged in his brain. He had not regained consciousness. The surgery would take several hours. The piece of steel would have to be extracted. The front portion of his forehead had been shattered. Once the surgery was completed, someone would come and let me know.

I was asked to sign papers to proceed. The wait turned out to be six hours.

The personality part of his brain, which is in the front, was completely destroyed, and the bone in his forehead was all cut away. He also lost his right eye. A tube was placed in his head for drainage; he would have to watched closely for infection.

Once out of surgery he was placed in ICU. We could not see him until the next day. I was numb at this point! It felt like I was walking in a dream. At any moment I would wake up and everything would be normal again. It is difficult to explain how you go through the motions of walking and talking, but you don't feel like it's your body. That is what I was feeling.

The next morning, we stopped at the nurse's station to ask for Stanley's room number, but before we went in, one of the doctors wanted to speak to me to explain his condition and what to expect. He was still unconscious and could remain in that state for a week, a month, or longer. There wasn't any way to tell how long it would be. When he did come to it was possible he would not know who we were. Since the portion of the brain removed was the personality part, the brain waves would have to rebuild themselves, which could take about a year; therefore, his personality would be different. Stanley would need to have extensive surgery to rebuild his eye and forehead. The surgeries would be spaced out about every three months. I was still numb, not believing all this was happening.

As we walked toward his room I felt sick to my stomach, mostly nerves. I hesitated a moment just before entering the room. He lay there so still, looking as though he was sleeping. If only that were the case. The only thing I could do was cry softly and not say a word. We didn't stay long.

The neighbors were so wonderful about helping take care of Janet. I couldn't say thank you enough! There was one problem. I did not have a driver's license. Asking someone to take me to the hospital every day was not something I could do. I had driven only a few times prior to this, so I asked a neighbor to go with me while I drove around the neighborhood to get a feel for driving again. After a short time, it came back to me. I said, "Okay, I'm ready to take the driving test." Everyone was shocked, but I was determined, and nothing was going to stand in my way. When it comes to push and shove, you do what you have to do and step up to the plate. The next day I took the drivers test and passed! My fear of driving in the city traffic disappeared. What a transformation! I know God was there every step of the way giving me the courage and ability. It was inside of me all the time; the will to do it overcame the fear.

In the days to come I had many mixed emotions; anger, and despair, and I kept asking God, "Why?" It was such a freak accident, this piece of steel flying all the way across the room and hitting Stanley in the eye. Of all the places it could have gone, why did he become the target? I could not see it at the time, but God was working in my life. He gave me strength and lifted me up to withstand the stress and tension I was experiencing.

When I could not pray I would sing. I found a song that became my rock: "I Know Who Holds Tomorrow." I would sing it over and over whenever I needed strength. I would go to my special place to talk to God and sing softly. I found comfort in the words. The song helped when I couldn't think of words to say.

You live life day today, and you don't know what will happen. But as long as you focus on God He knows what lies ahead. You will have gloomy days where skies can turn to gray, but the sun comes out again for better days. God says we are not to worry over things for He walks beside us all the way. As we trust in Jesus our burdens will get lighter. We may not understand many things, but the promise given by God is that He holds the future and is there to hold our hand through life's problems.

Two weeks later Stanley regained consciousness and was taken out of ICU. He didn't know who we were, and we tried many ways to bring back his memory. We would tell him things about his past in hopes that it would help him remember. Nothing seemed to work. I asked the doctor if I could bring his daughter to the hospital to see if that would bring any emotions. He agreed: they would bring Stanley into a waiting room, and I could bring Janet the next day. I remember telling Stanley, "This is your daughter," and putting her in his lap. Nothing happened! He didn't like holding her, and Janet began to cry. I picked her up and left. I did some crying myself.

Going to the hospital was very emotional. I felt I had to be strong and needed to hide my emotions. At home by myself I would cry a lot, still, trying to figure out why this had to happen.

He lost a lot of weight and wasn't eating very well. As time went on he began to eat better and get a little stronger. The doctor thought it might be better for him to go home; maybe this would help his memory. Preparations were made to take him home. Because he'd lost so much weight I had to buy him some new clothes. Before he was released, I was given instructions for his care.

Coming Home

The day Stanley was released from the hospital, the doctor asked me to come in and have a talk. He proceeded to explain a possible behavior change; because of the brain damage he would most likely have seizures. He was placed on a heavy dose of Dilantin and the doctor would moderate the dosage to try to keep him from having convulsions.

It was explained that I should not to expect him to remember the past. Time would let it happen. I should talk to him as I normally would. Whenever there is damage to the brain, especially the personality part, change occurs: he would not be the same person. I should also watch for any small pimples coming from the scar. That would mean infection had set in, and I was to call immediately. I should bring him back in two weeks for a check up.

The nurse brought a wheelchair into his room and wheeled Stanley out to the car. I told him, "You are going home." His expression was blank, and he didn't say anything—just looked at me. I got behind the wheel and took a deep breath. The road to recovery was going to be long, and I didn't have any idea what to expect. We would have to take it day by day.

It took a little time to get inside and into bed. When he walked, he just slid his feet and didn't lift up his legs. Some of the neighbors came outside when we drove up to wish him well; there wasn't any response from Stanley. He didn't have any idea of being married. It was more like I was someone taking care of him. He had no recognition that he was a husband or a father. He didn't talk, only said a few words when he was spoken to.

Then the hard part began. He had to be trained to walk, go to the bathroom, and feed himself, almost like a baby. It didn't take long, though. His brain had to be trained to do those things again. At the two-week checkup the doctor was impressed with his improvement. The only area where he had not improved was his memory. It would take time. The stitches were removed, and his next appointment was set for another two weeks.

The total responsibility of the household was now on my shoulders. I was in the position of head of household, caretaker, mother, and wife. It was overwhelming. Making decisions was difficult; there were times when I didn't know what to do. It was suggested to me to make a decision whether right or wrong, and don't worry about it.

This helped me in many ways. Sometimes you need a little push and encouragement; anytime I had to make a decision I always thought about what was said, and it became a way of helping me make choices.

Stanley was the one who had the injury, and he lost more that day than anyone else. But the thing was, he did not know what his loss was. In time he would gain a new personality. Little by little his memory would come back to a certain level but never like he was before the accident.

At night when everyone was asleep was the time I could meditate and pray. I still questioned why this had to happen; I didn't understand. At times I couldn't pray, so I would sing softly, then just sit and be still. Looking back on my childhood I was a loner, because of that, I believe I was able to be alone and ponder over my situation and learn to cope on my own. I was not the type to talk to councilors or clergy about how I felt or to pour out my problems. I managed to handle stress on my own; I might get depressed for a day but always came out of it. That is the strength God gave me. A friend gave me a book to read: *Why Bad Things Happen to Good People.* I'd recommend this to anyone who is going through an illness, death, or tough times. One thing that stuck with me is, God doesn't cause accidents to happen. If someone was walking down the street God does not say, "Okay, I'm going to have this brick fall on your head," or "You are going to be hit by a car." Accidents happen because of people, one way or another. God is there to help you through the trials and stress. On the other hand, I believe God tries to warn us of danger. When we have inner thoughts that something just doesn't feel right, listen to them. God is trying to tell us to beware. We should listen to our inner voice.

After three months at home Stanley's first surgery was scheduled to reconstruct the forehead. The procedure took bone from his hip and pieced it together to make a new structure for the forehead. The area was too large to put in a plate; it would be subjected to hot and cold.

After being home only a couple weeks from surgery I noticed a pimple coming out of the scar on his forehead. I called the hospital and left a message for the doctor, and he called back quickly. After I explained what was going on, instead of bringing him to the hospital, he would come by the house on his way home that night to take a look at it. I was impressed that someone so well known in the medical field would make a house call! He came over and, as soon as he looked at it, I was instructed to go ahead and take Stanley to the hospital. An infection had set in; a tube was placed in his forehead for it to drain out. He stayed for a week before the infection cleared up. Stanley had four more surgeries within the next two years, three on the eye, one to rebuild the eye socket, and another on his eyelid so he could have movement. Then a glass eye was fitted.

He had several seizures! I learned just by the way his eyes had this glazed look and his body would stiffen that a seizure was about to occur. During a seizure the jaw sets really rigidly, and the mouth closes. I used a spoon to hold down his tongue to keep him from biting it.

Another Trauma

Father's Day, June 1963, we received a phone call from my family telling us that my younger sister, Johnice, had been in an automobile accident. She had severe injuries, and we should come. Hanging up, I was numb. Another accident! What next? The next day we packed up and drove to the hospital. In silence I was praying, "Lord you have said you would not give us more than we could ever handle, but this time Lord I don't know if I'm going to be strong enough."

My sister had gone to a neighboring town to see a movie. Entering into town you crossed over double railroad tracks, equipped only with lights to stop traffic when trains approached. Witnesses told the police that it appeared the lights were not working when they saw the car go across the tracks. What she didn't see, until it was too late, was a freight train fast approaching; the train whistle blew, and within seconds the train hit her car. The impact was on the side where my sister was sitting. The train dragged the car until it finally flipped away from the tracks, throwing my sister out. She slid a hundred yards, hitting her head against a brick building. When the ambulance arrived she was still breathing. She was rushed to a hospital in Springfield, Missouri, about sixty miles away.

Afterwards the family learned that she was in really bad shape and the doctors weren't sure if she would make it. Once she arrived at the hospital she was immediately packed in ice to bring down her temperature. Her head was swollen to twice its normal size, and she had some broken bones; there was hardly a place on her body that wasn't skinned.

Walking into the hospital my thoughts went back to just a little over a year ago. Then it was Stanley I was going to see, now it was my sister. I knew my folks were going to be grief stricken. Again I needed to be strong for them.

She was in the ICU unit; only one family member could go in at a time. As I walked into the room my body felt clammy; I didn't want to look at her, afraid of what I would see.

Tears swelled in my eyes. She was still packed in ice, and the doctors could not do anything until her temperature came down. The skin had to heal before bones could be set. She was unconscious and looked really bad.

She remained packed in ice for three days; her temperature went down to an acceptable level, and slowly the swelling of her head began to recede; then she regained consciousness.

Of course she did not remember anything, which is normal for anyone that has gone through a trauma. She remained in the hospital for three months. She had a huge gash on her right leg just above the knee where the car ashtray cut her leg. Another problem was that she couldn't walk. There wasn't much encouragement that she would ever walk again. This was not acceptable for my parents. After they brought her home they worked with her legs and feet by lifting and exercising them every four hours. They did this day in and day out, never giving up on the idea of her walking again.

As time passed she began to get stronger. She was able to take a few steps, then use a walker, until one day she walked all on her own. It was Mother and Dad's faith in God, believing she would be healed, and their commitment to keep working with her therapy, never giving up. That is the reason she is walking today. God works miracles every day.

After two and half years all Stanley's surgeries were completed, and he was released from the doctor's care. His memory had been slow in coming back. He remembered most everything. His personality was different.

The best thing for us was to move near family; I still needed some support. We put our house on the market, and it sold rather quickly. Times were tough, financially and emotionally. Stanley still did not show any emotion as husband or father. He could not work, and our only income was his disability check, which wasn't much. This meant I would have to go to work. My only work experience was in high school. During the summer months I worked at Newberry's Five & Dime Store.

I remember my high school summer job very well because my transportation to and from work was unique. We lived in the country, about eight miles from town. Neither of my parents could take me to work, so I had to find a way to get there. There was a commuter train, kind of rickety, to say the least. Its only function was to transport people from one town to another: a twenty-five-mile trek. If you wanted to ride the train, the method of stopping it was to stand at a designated area and wave a white flag. The conductor would see the flag and stop to pick you up. If I remember correctly, the cost was only twenty-five cents each way.

Once we were settled I started looking for employment.

My Angels

The one thing that kept me grounded and gave me purpose was my children. The person I married had changed. Many things changed: his personality and his ability to work at his profession, not to mention his emotions. He continued not to recognize his role as father and husband. I had a lot of stress trying to cope with the reality of all this. I found comfort and joy in the love of my daughters; they helped me get through each day.

Janet was only eighteen months old when Stanley's accident happened; she had some of my childhood traits, shy and timid. She became very attached to her mother; that was understandable because she was the one thing I could cling to for comfort. I know I spoiled her a lot. Although Janet was shy, she was also curious and liked to explore. One thing she learned well was climbing. One day while playing she seemed really quiet.

When I went to check on her she was sitting on the floor eating baby aspirins. There was a full bottle in the kitchen cabinet, and she had climbed upon the cabinet to get to them and climbed down again. How she was able to open the bottle is still a mystery. Anyway, she had eaten several aspirins. I immediately called the doctor. She had to be taken to the emergency room and have her stomach pumped. What a nightmare! This had been Janet's second time to climb up on the cabinet. The first time she decided to mix my flour and coffee together that were in canisters on the counter top. I found out how she was climbing up. She would pull out the bottom drawer, and climb from there onto the counter. I couldn't classify her as a terrible two, but she was adventurous and quick.

It had been four years since Stanley's accident. At this point I was pretty tense and held in a lot of stress. Muscles around my shoulders and neck were really tight. After consulting the family doctor, I was put on a muscle relaxant, which helped, but it didn't take away the stress.

Stanley finally accepted the role of being married, but he still didn't behave like a husband or father; this was part of the emotional stress. I still made all the decisions as head of the household, including all the parenting decisions. My feelings for him were not the same either; he was not the person I fell in love with and married. I never knew how he felt.

While he was still under the doctor's care, it was discussed that we might not be able to have more children. But, this proved to be wrong. I became pregnant, and our second child, Ronda, was born August 14, 1966.

A newborn baby is the most precious thing; they are loveable, sweet, and cuddly. They depend on you for their every need. Now, I had a new focus. Ronda was born on a Sunday, which to me was God's way of saying she was a special child born on a special day. My heart overflowed with love and joy for this child. I felt so blessed! Having another baby was the greatest gift I could receive. She was an easy birth and a good baby to care for. Janet also loved her baby sister; I think she was good for both of us. I let Janet help in ways she was capable of; I did not want to make her feel unloved or to be jealous. To make it a special occasion for Janet we bought her a red bike as a celebration of the birth of her new sister.

Our house sat directly across the street from the elementary school; all you had to do was walk across the street and onto the school grounds. How convenient! You would think nothing could go wrong. School began the first Monday after Labor Day. Ronda was almost three weeks old, and Janet had just turned six. It was her first day of school. She was all excited! I told her I would walk her over to help find her classroom. I picked Ronda up, and we headed out the door. As we were walking across the street I explained to Janet that when she got out of school not to cross the street by herself, but to wait for me. I would be standing in the front yard watching for her and would come to get her. She said okay. We found her room, and I waited until she settled in before I went back home.

Stanley had acquired a job as janitor; his ability to work at any other profession wasn't possible. With a new baby I needed to be at home.

Time came for school to be over for the day. I picked Ronda up and went out into the front yard to watch for Janet. I knew it would be a little wait, but

I expected to see her before the busses pulled out. Soon the busses started going by the house one by one, and I grew a little apprehensive; Janet should have come out. After they were gone I stood and watched; no Janet. I panicked! My heart started beating faster, and I dashed over to the school and found her teacher. We looked all over, but did not find her. Perhaps she got on a bus by mistake. A call was made to the high school for help in locating her. I was instructed to go home and wait for a phone call and try to stay calm; she would be found. I was almost in tears. My legs felt like lead trying to walk home. I didn't know if I could make it, but I did. At home I paced the floor waiting for the call. After about twenty minutes the phone rang. I received a call saying they found her. She got on the bus with her friend. Because her friend rode the bus, Janet wanted to also. When they stopped at the high school, Janet went up and told the driver he passed her house. She explained where she lived, and he began to laugh. She was taken to the principal's office, and the story was told. Everyone laughed.

Anyway, she would be brought home as soon as the busses left the school grounds. I was relieved by their laughter, and I too began to see the humor in it and relaxed. I didn't realize it, but I had become so weak in the knees I fell onto the sofa. When she returned home, I did not punish her; rather, I explained to her in a stern, motherly voice not to do that again. I took her in my arms and hugged her for a longtime.

Happy are the memories of not so long ago; I find daily happiness in remembering all the little things and the love in my heart for my daughters. They gave me strength to face each day and were my reason for living.

Single Years

After twelve years of marriage, I filed for divorce. It was the most difficult thing I have ever done. It took me one year to get up the courage. The last six months we slept in separate bedrooms. I felt guilty; as far as my religious beliefs you married for life. I was so stressed and tense I went to see a doctor. I was given a prescription to help calm my nerves, and a question was asked of me: who do you want to raise your children? Of course I wanted to be the one to do that. I was given something to think about, although I was scared to death, wondering if I could earn enough money to support us.

Before I filed for divorce, something happened that made me realize I must make some changes. A friend invited me to go to the lake for a boat ride and get a little R&R. I never went out to do anything by myself. I initially declined but was persuaded to go. I found someone to stay with the girls. It was a beautiful day! I remember the water being crystal clear, calm, and like glass. You could see you reflection. Staring at the water I thought how easy it would be just to slip over the side and end it all; my problems would be over.

Then I saw the faces of my girls, and at that moment I silently asked God to forgive me. I would never leave my girls; they were my life. My eyes filled with tears; and I sat there letting the breeze fill my face as we speed along the water. I never mentioned this to anyone.

Many people stay in relationships for fear of not having the ability to take care of themselves financially. With God all things are possible. I thank God for opening doors of opportunity for me. Single life isn't easy. The key is to trust in God and be open minded to new things. He was with me all the way.

Jesus in my life, giving me the will and strength to survive as a single parent and provider, is the reason for my success.

Change happens all the time; accept it and go forward. You will understand as I go through my employment process; I started at the bottom and worked up to better myself.

This was a time of fear and uncertainty. Throughout the next few years I would surprise myself. I stood up to challenges, grew emotionally, and became determined to better myself. Through the Grace of God I became more than I thought I could be. When I accepted Jesus into my heart at an early age, I was given God's grace that would be with me always. What amazed me, was that although I was a little on the shy side, I overcame this obstacle and became an independent person.

A clothing store opened in town, and since I had previous retail experience I applied for a job. In my interview I expressed my desire to work up in the company to a management position. This made a good impression! I was hired, and within three months I was promoted to assistant manager. This company had several stores in the state, and my potential to move up the ladder was there.

I made many wrong choices in marriage and relationships. I should have taken the time to see what was the right thing for me as well as for my children. It was immaturity on my part, to say the least.

The clothing store I worked for had an opening at a store only twenty-five miles from my parent's home. I asked if I could be considered for store manager, and to my surprise the position was offered to me. I was overjoyed!

Over the next few years my lifestyle changed. I was looking for love in all the wrong places in pursuit of more worldly things in life. Realizing this wasn't the life for me, I needed to work on changing my behavior. I also learned some things about myself. I made a vow that I was not going to get involved again. Marriage was out of the question, at least not until the girls had completed school and were on their own.

I began to read self-help books and anything else along that line. I didn't forget my faith in God; I just needed to re-gain that faith. I became fascinated with the reincarnation theory. It made sense that you come back in other lives to improve yourself in order to obtain perfection. I bought that for a while, but couldn't find scriptures to back up this theory. It took awhile for me to find an explanation of the real purpose of life. I heard a sermon one Sunday that our purpose on this earth is to serve God and to tell others of His love.

The most important thing for me was raising my girls and establishing my career; everything else had to wait. We lived on a tight budget. When the girls turned sixteen and wanted their own car, I explained to them if this is what you want you will have to pay for the car, insurance, and gas money, which means they would have to get a job. In the long run it taught them to manage money and responsibility. It wasn't easy being a single mom; there were times when the girls gave me problems. At those times I just didn't want to be a mom anymore. That didn't last long, thank goodness; everything has a way of working out.

Healing from my last relationship took some time. I took a job at the local library. The pay was meager, and being on my own meant I needed to find a job that would support us. In looking over the want ads in the local newspaper I noticed a position open for advertising sales. Since most of my background was in sales I applied. The paper was a weekly edition. I had a good rapport with my interviewer and was hired.

My duties were in outside sales for large display ads. This turned out to be a fun job and brought out some of my inner abilities I didn't know existed. My creative side emerged. I learned very quickly and how to layout ads. I'd create promotional ideas and ad campaigns. Since it was a small weekly paper, everyone had to help put the paper together: type set, paste up, and proofread. Usually it was midnight by the time the paper was put to bed. It was the greatest feeling at the end of an exhausting day knowing that tomorrow many people would be reading what you had a part in making happen. Each time I went into a new job, I could visualize things that needed improvement, or ways the business could be improved. In retail I knew how to dress up the windows to draw customers into the store, and I created promotional ideas. For the newspaper I turned out creative promotional ads for my customers, and even won a couple awards.

Two years later, a position was posted in the classified section for Director of the Chamber of Commerce. Sometimes you just have to believe in yourself and go for it even thought you think your qualifications might not be strong enough. I didn't know if I would qualify but went in for an interview anyway. It came down to another person and me for the position. Sadly the other person was hired. Six months later this person resigned, and I was called back for a second interview, and this time the job was mine.

The main industry was tourism, and the majority of the function of the chamber was dealing with resorts/motels and tourist related business. This turned out to be one of my best jobs. It was full of enjoyment.

My experience at the newspaper proved to be an asset for this position. The Chamber of Commerce published an entertainment directory and lodging magazine each year. They were distributed in the office, at all businesses in the area, and at the off-season I attended boat and travel shows promoting our area. January, February, and March was the season for shows, traveling throughout four states. It was a lot of fun meeting people from all over the United States and Canada who also promoted their tourist destinations. I drove to most of the boat-show locations. I didn't have any problem reading maps, and I had a good sense of direction. I did have one bad experience coming home from the show in Wichita, Kansas. I drove a blue, four-cylinder Mazda. The size fit me fine, and it got good gas mileage. I left Wichita around four p.m. on a Sunday afternoon and about an hour down the road my car began to register hot. I slowed down and began looking for a place to stop to get some water. I knew I couldn't drive very long before I would need to stop. Soon I saw a house on the right side of the road. I stopped and asked for water. I was given a plastic milk jug. I filled it with water and put the water in my car.

I took the milk jug in case I needed it later. The next town was thirty miles further down the road. I was very appreciative of the help. I got back in my car and drove on. I don't think I drove more than ten miles before it started getting hot again. I looked at the side of the road for water and spotted some in the ditch. I stopped and filled up with water. I slowly drove down the road and it took over an hour to make it to the next town. I saw a Chevrolet dealership and pulled into their lot. They were closed! I looked around and there was a motel across the street. I left my car in the parking lot, picked up my suitcase and walked across the street. I told the motel clerk about my situation and got a little sympathy.

The next morning, as soon as the dealership opened I walked across. After exchanging information the car was inspected. The problem was major. My motor had cracked! Another decision! After looking at my options I needed some time to think. I went back to my room and prayed about my situation. What was the best choice? I could leave my car and have it repaired and return to pick it up later. The repair was expensive! I could sell the car and go home, then purchase another used car. Since my car was paid off I was in a better position. I ended up selling my car. God was with me. I was able to find a ride to Wichita and flew to Kansas City. I called a friend to come and pick me up at the airport. I was amazed that I managed to stay calm and didn't panic throughout this ordeal. Once I arrived home I did find another used car. I thanked God for guiding the way and helping me stay calm.

During the drive I had a lot of time to think and a vision came to me for the Chamber.

In the area there were two Chambers of Commerce only a couple miles apart, each governed by a Board of Directors. Ours was a full-service chamber, the other one operated an information booth, handing out brochures and giving referrals for lodging and entertainment. The vision was to merge the two chambers to make one stronger organization instead of competing with each other for the same goal. I presented my idea at the monthly meeting. We did not know if the other chamber would consider it, so it was tabled. I knew in my heart it would be a good thing.

I began to stop at businesses in both areas and discussed the idea with the owners. I explained how it would benefit them, and I helped shape their opinions. After two months it was brought up that we should meet with the other Chamber to discuss a merger. It wasn't long before it did happen. It turned out to be the best thing for the community. It became a stronger force in promoting the area as a whole.

The experience I gained from this job was memorable in many ways: I still reflect back on it as some of the best times of my life. What a joy it was to work in an environment like that.

The position gave me notoriety in the community; it's something I valued. I was also involved in other community organizations.

Another accomplishment we could take some credit for was getting a new bridge built across the lake. The main highway crossed over the lake; the bridge was over fifty years old and was beginning to deteriorate; chunks of cement were breaking off and falling. I began writing letters to state representatives and senators asking for their help in obtaining funds to rebuild the bridge. They responded quickly saying this bridge was on a list of one hundred bridges to be replaced. I wrote to the highway commissioner pleading our case to him. With all the tourists coming into the area we have more traffic crossing the bridge than other areas. It was unsafe, and it would be devastating for the state if the unthinkable would happen. It really needed to be priority! Correspondence went on for about a year. A selected group went to the state capitol to lobby for the bridge funds.

This was interesting and an unforgettable experience. Finally the funds were approved, and a new bridge was built.

The dedication was on August 31, 1984. This was an election year. President Ronald Regan was in office and up for re-election. I had to make plans for the dedication and my thought, because this was an election year, was that perhaps I could get the president to come for the dedication speech. I wrote a letter to the White House and received a response rather quickly; unfortunately, due to other commitments he could not honor our request. I still was elated. I had received a letter from the White House!

There was a lot of excitement on the day of the dedication when a telegram came for me. I received a call at the office telling me there was a telegram from President Regan sending greetings for the dedication.

A funny thing happened just before the dedication began, although it wasn't funny at the time! I wore an A-line skirt, and while I was waiting on the bridge for the ceremony to begin, along with a few other dignitaries, a wasp flew up my skirt and stung me on the leg just above the knee. I didn't know what it was. I couldn't pull up my skirt to see, so with my hand I grasped the area where the sting occurred and could feel the wasp. I squashed it and let it fall onto the ground. I was in a lot of pain! Other than the person standing next to me, no one else knew what had happened. I had to stand there during the whole program and grit my teeth and bear it. As soon as the program was over, I ran to my car and raced home, which wasn't too far; I mixed some baking soda with water to put on it; by this time the whelp was pretty big and red!

This event was my last day with the Chamber of Commerce. I found myself at another turning point. Both of my daughters had moved to Houston, Texas. Janet married and left six years earlier, Ronda joined her a few months after graduating. I thought, why am I staying here? Plus, Janet had my first grandchild; I wanted to live close enough to enjoy him. Every grandparent knows what I mean when I say that one of the greatest pleasures is being a grandparent. What a joy! Texas was too far away from Missouri, so I packed up and moved.

My first few jobs in Houston were in newspaper and retail. the pay was not good, so I began to search for a new field of work. Looking over the want ads I keep seeing a lot of available jobs in the hotel market, although most wanted experience. The majority of my work experience was sales related; I put my resume together with a strong emphasis on sales and marketing. I lived in the north area of Houston near the airport; there were several hotels. I hand delivered my resume to ten hotels, and soon after I received a call from a hotel to come in for an interview. I was hired and stayed there for a couple years. I enjoyed the hotel business, but the downside was a lot of hours. It was a good learning experience; now I had new qualifications to add to my resume: catering and sales.

I moved on to another job at a country club as food and beverage manager. During my seven years at this job I also served as the membership director. I loved the atmosphere, catering to the members, trying to service their needs, and overseeing golf tournaments, banquets, and wedding receptions. Although this was a demanding position I enjoyed this type of work. I had to work six days a week; my only day off was Monday. This was the longest I had stayed at any one job, and since I worked on Sundays I did not go to church. Again I distance myself from God. After seven years of working all the time, I had burned out. I really needed a change. One important thing was going back to church to find my way back into God's Grace.

This time I decided to try going into business for myself and open a tearoom. It didn't work out! Within the next four years I worked at three different jobs before I considered retirement. Retirement looked like a good option. This was the end of one journey and the beginning of a new one.

Being a single female can be tough at times. Fortunately, on the other hand, life can be rewarding. I remember buying my first home as a single person. It was a scary process, but after closing, that scary feeling disappeared. Throughout the years, I have bought four homes and sold three. My last home was brand new. I call it my retirement home.

While living in my third home, I came to another crossroad. I needed a large sum of money, and thought I had home equity to use. I looked into a reverse mortgage, but that wasn't the best solution. My second option was to borrow against the equity, and a third option was to sell the home. When struggling to make a decisions, I like to walk and silently talk to God. I believe in turning my problems over to God and trust He will show me the best way. So I walked! I prayed, saying, "God, I put this in your hands. As doors open I will know the direction I should go." It became very clear that the best plan was to sell. I contacted a realtor to place it on the market. After two weeks the house sold; within thirty days we closed on the house. This was unexpected to sell so quickly; I had figured on about six months. Now I knew God had a hand in this! I had to get in high gear and look for another home. Just by accident, one day while out looking at homes, I wandered into a new sub-division. This happened to be my lucky day. By the end of the week I had bought a new home. This was a blessing from God. To honor Him I decided to have my home blessed. I made plans to have a house blessing instead of an open house. A program was planned and invitations made. It turned out to be a beautiful service. Family and friends came and helped celebrate my new home.

Stanley died from a brain tumor in the Fall of 1996.

A New Journey

There are many forks in the road of life; mine was about to take another road. The time for me to make a choice: should I retire or keep working? God has a way of guiding us in our thoughts if we listen. I prayed about it, and made a list of the pros and cons. The direction was quite clear; after a lot of thought I chose to retire.

What do I do with my life now that I have all this free time? I could sleep late; there would not be an alarm clock waking me up for work. I'd have more time to spend with family and friends. This was a new chapter in my life. I welcome changes; I keep an open mind and go forward with the attitude that tomorrow good things are in store for me. A passage in Isaiah, 42:9, says, "Behold, the former things have come to pass, and new things I now declare."

Now that I have time I can take up a hobby. As a young girl I learned to embroider and spent a lot of time making kitchen towels and pillowcases. During the cold winter months, mother would have a quilt set up, and my sisters and I helped with the quilting. We did not have a TV so we spent our spare time sewing. Now was a good time for me to use those skills once again. I began making quilts. I purchased preprinted quilt blocks to embroider and then hand quilted the quilts. I found this to be relaxing and I felt a lot of pride once the quilt was completed.

Both daughters had a family vacation planned, and now that I had all this free time I was invited to go with each of their vacations in the fall. Another trip I had to plan was to visit my mother and family in Missouri; the discussion was to wait until spring; that way Janet, Ronda, and their children could go. God had a hand in making this decision, which we would come to understand after the trip. It was the last time I had to visit with my older sister. In loving memory her strong faith inspired us all.

Have you ever experienced a time or moment where you felt God prepared the way? I have had a few of those.

There was an incident when I discovered God's timing was perfect. One Christmas both Janet and Ronda were going out of town over the holidays, and they didn't want me to spend Christmas alone. Plans were made for me to take a two-day holiday trip to St. Paul, Minnesota. I had a friend who lived there, and it would be great to visit with her.

Before they purchased the ticket they did tell me about the trip to make sure it was fine with me. Of course it was! A dream of mine was to go to the Mall of America. There were other historical sites to see, but it was doubtful there would be enough time, flying up one day, only having one full day, then the third day flying back home. Another trip, another time!

The day I arrived it was cold, and they had recently had a big snowstorm. Snow was piled up against the buildings and where sidewalks had been cleared. At least I was used to cold and snow, although not to this extent. I did have the right clothing with me.

The next day my dream came true; here I was at Mall of America. I was totally amazed! There was so much to see and all the shops; it's a good thing I had on comfortable shoes. Most of the day was spent at the mall. I can say I enjoyed every minute.

This was the last time to see my friend. Later I learned she had a terminal illness.

Proud Grandparent

I cannot write about my life without mentioning my grandchildren. They bring the greatest joy into my daily life. Janet had my first grandson, Christopher. Later on after a divorce she married Scott. He had three boys whom he had custody of: John, Jimmy, and Michael. Ronda married Greg and they have two children: Matthew and Laura (my first granddaughter). There is an age difference of fourteen years between Janet's son and Ronda's children.

When Chris was a small boy I visualized him going into the military when he grew up, which was a fearful thought. It wasn't surprising when he decided, at the age of eighteen, to join the Army. Serving his time in the military would give him the opportunity to have his college paid for and, at the same time earn an income for the next four years. My first thought was, at least we are not in a war, and perhaps he can get his four years in without any war time. Sadly this was not the case; he joined two months before September 11, 2001. What was to follow is history. All of our fears turned into reality; the war with Iraq was to come.

Chris's Boot Camp was in Oklahoma, and after he graduated was transferred to South Carolina until he was shipped to Germany for his permanent base. Germany was his choice because he studied the German language in high school, and wanted to test his language skills in that country. He was able to do some traveling while living there, visiting other countries. He probably would never have had the opportunity if not for the military.

At home we all held our breath each day expecting to receive the call that he would be sent to Iraq: that moment came a couple years later. What a horrible feeling in the pit of my stomach. All I could think about was, he is too young to be in this situation. I only saw him as a young boy and not the man he became. Just thinking about the age of all the soldiers and how young they were was almost unreal for me. Every time the news broadcasted reports about Iraq I would stop in my tracks and race to the TV, my heart pounding, waiting to hear the information. One such broadcast told about the city where Chris's base was located; it had been attacked at the gate, where a battle ensued. The attackers withdrew, but five men in his unit were injured or killed. We later found out Chris and another solider had to pick them up in a vehicle. His job was mechanic and driver; he was responsible for keeping the vehicles running. Whenever they went out on patrol it was dangerous because they always had to be on the lookout for hidden explosives buried along the roadside.

I never went to bed without praying for Chris's safety, and when I woke in the morning, I said another prayer. I asked God to wrap his arms around Chris to keep him safe and to give him angles to watch over him. He was in my thoughts every day. It was during this year that I became spiritually closer to God.

After a year in Iraq he was released to return to Germany; at this time he only had a few months left for his tenure in the Army. His discharge was July 2005. All we could say was, "Praise the Lord!" He came through without any injuries. At last he was a civilian once again; time now to adjust to a normal lifestyle.

Chris kept a journal during his time in Iraq, writing as often as possible. I asked if I could read it. Reading about his daily life gave me a broad sense of what it was like living there for that one year. There were a lot of bad days, some dangerously bad, and rarely a good day. We (family members) sent him care packages while on his tour of duty; what he asked for were food items. I knew he loved olives; at the grocery store I discovered packages of olives in plastic bags, each bag contained around twenty-five to thirty olives. These were a favorite.

As I reflect back to when my father was in World War II (I was only five years old at the time) I wonder how mother got through it. She didn't have the Internet to keep in touch like we did, or a telephone to call when she wanted to. The only way to communicate was through letters, and then it took weeks to receive mail. TV wasn't invented; the radio was the only news provider. After my dad came home from the war, he would not talk about what happened or what he saw. It was too painful to remember. He wanted to forget.

The stage of life for me now that I am a senior citizen is entirely different. I have been single for several years, retired, and enjoying life. Today I can say I'm happy with who I am; being single doesn't matter. I feel at peace and am satisfied with my life.

I want to leave you with this thought: "We are never alone." Learn from your past and keep looking toward God for guidance. Let us remember He is All Powerful and has endless mercy. Keep an open mind, and try new things.